Beyond

Beyond Survival

Practical Hope in Powerful Times

by Graham Leicester

with artwork by Jennifer Williams

tp

Published in this first edition in 2020 by:

Triarchy Press
Axminster, UK

www.triarchypress.net

Copyright © International Futures Forum, 2020

The right of Graham Leicester to be identified as the author of
this work has been asserted by him in accordance with the
Copyright, Designs and Patents Act, 1988

A catalogue record for this book is available from the British
Library.

ISBNs
Print: 978-1-913743-03-1
ePub: 978-1-913743-04-8
PDF: 978-1-913743-05-5

Artwork by Jennifer Williams

**Jennifer Williams is critically acclaimed at making hand-made
books, cut-outs, photographs, illustrations, prints and
puppets. She is a trustee and member of International
Futures Forum and for 31 years directed the Centre for
Creative Communities.**

Printed by TJ International, Padstow, Cornwall

Contents

Introduction: Practical Hope

"Hell is a most popular subject today because so many people are in it. Hell is very stimulating and easy to understand. Paradise is very difficult to understand, and also, there is in Paradise a rebuke. In that Paradise there is a purity which reveals one's own sense of impurity."

Cecil Collins, visionary artist and educator,
Theatre of the Soul, 1979

This is a powerful moment in powerful times. I write in the midst of a global pandemic that has already claimed more than 300,000 lives and leaves billions more across the world living in mortal fear. It has tipped the already precarious into destitution and threatens to leave an economic and a moral wound[1] from which we will struggle to recover.

That we saw this coming offers no relief. In fact, quite the opposite: the impact is inevitably tinged with hints of blame and shame at the warnings that went unheeded. Yet in truth

---

[1] Our actions and inactions during this crisis, the decisions we have had to make, the loneliness of separation we have imposed – including on the dying, the ways in which we have seen others behave and we have behaved ourselves, the negative consequences of the measures we have taken to mitigate the immediate impact of the disease, the suffering we have witnessed and the agonising question as to whether we could have done more to prevent it – these are sources even now of moral pain, a pain that will endure.

we have for years been living in a world threatened by considerably more than four horsemen of the apocalypse and a veritable flock of black swans coming home to roost.

All of these threats are systemically interconnected (as we are now discovering afresh) and somewhere near the top of the risk register lies the ominous phrase "failure of global governance". The 21st-century emergency is both real (there are consequences), conceptual (horribly complex to understand and to grasp in its multiple dimensions) and existential (shaking the inner foundations of our worlds).

This pamphlet updates one I first published during the last big worldwide systemic shock – the near-collapse of the financial system in 2008. Like many others at that time I was keen to support the opportunity the crisis offered to rethink finance and its place in the world system, to rebuild on new principles, fit for the future.

Today's shock has been more wide-ranging and substantial. It has had a more immediate and more profound impact than any other recent critical event on the many interconnected aspects of our world system. The same impulse to repattern the world rather than return to the dangerous path of the old normal has again been expressed, this time with more urgency, more depth of feeling and more ambition.

Even so, it would be easy to look back to 2008 and what has happened since, and indeed to previous pivotal moments in history, and conclude that however great our desire to rebuild anew, the old order is remarkably resilient, has not left the field, is able to absorb temporary defeats and will come back stronger and more sure of its worldview than ever. How can we best work to ensure that things turn out differently this time around – not least as we look ahead to other challenges looming on the horizon?

The thread weaving through these four essays is hope – practical hope. Raymond Williams tells us that our task is "to make hope possible rather than despair convincing". But for me hope is *always* possible. The real challenge at this point is to make it *convincing*. Then it might attract the resources to match our ambitions and, just as 'lockdown' has proved a more or less global immediate response to the pandemic, hope might frame for everyone the invigorating spirit of the next phase – recovery and renewal.

Despair is more alluring. 'The devil always has the best tunes.' The hopeful story, by contrast, touches a precious place in us and is more demanding of the listener. It is easier to dismiss visionary alternatives as unrealistic and utopian than to acknowledge, as Cecil Collins suggests in the epigraph above, that their very imagining represents a challenge to who we are, what we regard as living, and what we are prepared to stand for today.

We can learn lessons from the rich history of hope in action in periods of challenge and duress. Those who emerge from crisis with both their aspirations and their humanity intact appear to draw on a number of common resources.

The first resource is **survival**. For now, most of us have retreated into our homes to protect ourselves - collectively - from the virus. But outside the world has changed and to re-enter it, find our accommodation with it, realise our dreams within it, we will have to make sense of it afresh – we will need **insight**.

This is no quick fix – even as we dream of a vaccine and a cure. There will be other challenges ahead and other forces set to thwart us. The journey from survival to insight to action to realisation is going to take time and **perseverance**. Which points to the importance of **hope**, the most *vital* resource in every sense, without which we cannot even start the journey.

We will need to draw upon strengths and inner resources we may not think we have and that our typical defensive response to crisis denies us. These resources are not technical or structural or theoretical: they are existential. It is our artists, our poets, our myth-makers who have constantly brought them to mind for us for generations.

One touchstone for me is Seamus Heaney's extraordinary acceptance speech for his 1995 Nobel prize for literature. In it he tells of his own experience of losing hope during the "harrowing of the heart" that he experienced through the years of conflict in his native Northern Ireland. He describes how during that period for decades he bent over his desk like a monk, going through the motions of writing, "blowing up sparks for meagre heat".

But then "finally and happily" he "straightened up". He found his inner strength again. As he puts it: "I began... to try to make space in my reckoning and imagining for the marvellous as well as for the murderous".

Heaney illustrates the point with a story about a group of workmates ambushed by the roadside in those times. The armed gunmen line the men up against a wall and ask that any Catholic amongst them step forward. The assumption is that these are Protestant paramilitaries, and that the Catholics will be shot dead.

The one Catholic amongst them, "caught between dread and witness", makes a motion to step forward. But at that moment, in the darkness, he feels the Protestant worker next to him take his hand and squeeze it, as if to say – don't worry, we will not betray you, stay in line. But it is too late. He has already made a motion. He expects to be shot, but instead is thrown aside as the rest of the men are gunned down. The gunmen themselves are Catholic, presumably members of the Provisional IRA.

The image haunts Heaney – as it must anyone who reads his speech. It is a reminder of the utter inseparability of the marvellous and the murderous, both ever present and always available in the same image. The squeeze of the hand is as real as the volley of gunfire, and as much a part of our human nature.

Yet, as Heaney puts it, "as writers and readers, as sinners and citizens, our realism and our aesthetic sense make us wary of crediting the positive note." It is the gift of poetry, in particular what he calls "the necessary poetry", to lend power to the positive, to hold both the murderous and the marvellous "in a single thought".

As we contemplate dark times ahead, we too must be open to the marvellous, ready to see and to respond to hope amidst despair. Not false hope, not blithe optimism, not the fantasy of rescue, but the mature hope that brings with it its own burden, its own challenge.

Heaney concludes his essay by pointing to the contradictory needs we experience at times of crisis: "the need on the one hand for a truth telling that will be hard and retributive, and on the other hand, the need not to harden the mind to a point where it denies its own yearnings for sweetness and trust."

In view of the dark imaginings that crowd in on us today, and the inevitable sense of a grim and necessary reckoning ahead, the few words of practical hope that follow are offered in that spirit.

Lesson One: Survival

"Batten down the hatches – there's rough seas ahead!" Sage and timeless advice, even for those of us who are not sailors. We know what it means. Secure the vessel, make sure it's watertight. Then head below and pray it will hold us through the storm. The first priority is survival.

Those who really know about survival, including survival at sea, will tell you there is more to it than that. Better to leave at least one person on deck, lashed to the tiller, watching for a break in the weather, 'steering' as best they can and tugging on the storm jib.

Think of Gericault's dramatic painting of *The Raft of the Medusa* with its mass of ship-wrecked, writhing bodies clinging to a panel from the sinking ship. Our eyes are drawn to the one brave soul up on his feet, straining his body to scan the horizon, waving desperately at a distant sail.

Studies of accidents, plane crashes, shipwrecks, people who get lost in the wilderness etc show that those who decide to sit still and wait for things to get better are more likely to perish. The first rule for survivors is to 'discard the hope of rescue'. Survival, like hope, is an action and those who act are more likely to survive.

But what kind of action? Typically, crisis response, both at an individual and a societal or community level, follows a familiar pattern. The immediate impact places a natural focus on the safety of self, friends, family, colleagues. Make sure the vessel is watertight. This is essential. But beyond this initial instinctive impulse it pays to become more circumspect.

There is always a vigorous, adrenaline-fuelled early response: working all hours, doing whatever it takes. In a crisis people, and institutions, tend to become more intense versions of themselves – the anxious panic, the energetic get hyperactive, governments turn to command and control, health services leave their person-centred fringe and go full-on medical tech in order to restore order and save lives. The activity can take on a manic quality, an unconscious defence against anxiety.

This is also the time when rumours start to circulate. They serve as largely unconscious ways to process our strong emotions: scapegoat rumours to channel our frustration, bogie man rumours and conspiracy theories to channel our fears, pipe-dream rumours to offer us hope.

One manual for disaster relief workers laconically describes this initial phase as "characterized by a high level of activity with a low level of productivity". Like the drowning person thrashing about in a cold sea when the survival advice is the opposite: lie back, regain control of your breathing, "float to live".

Survival schools echo this first requirement to stabilise and come to our senses. They use the acronym STOP: stop, think, observe, plan… and then, crucially, act. The stop phase involves calming down, breathing normally, floating rather than thrashing about.

In this way we restore our capacity to think, which is critical to survival and much more difficult than you would imagine. Even at the best of times our thoughts are accompanied by feelings and our emotions condition our thinking. We are more likely to see what we believe than believe what we see.

All the more so when we are in danger, under pressure, or anxious. Highly charged emotion and deeper psychological currents of fear and dread will crowd out rational thought. People who wander off the trail and get lost almost never turn back. They press on, convincing themselves that they are still on track and will come across a landmark just around the next corner. This is called 'bending the map'.

Regaining 'cognitive control', coming to our senses, is critical. That is why the emergency services, trained to respond to crisis with clear heads in the face of strong emotions, set up levels of command – operational, tactical, strategic – such that the strategic level is shielded from the emotional charge of being in the thick of it. The rest of us try to achieve the same effect by not reading the newspapers or turning off the social media feed. As Eliot said, 'Human kind cannot bear very much reality'.

Government tends to turn to the military. They have been trained to act dispassionately in crisis situations: how else could they pull the trigger in time of war? Fighter pilots have intensive training to cope with things going wrong at high speed. They are drilled to the point where the right thing to do becomes instinctive even when the body is suffused with fear. As one instructor says, "when you climb inside the cockpit your IQ rolls back to that of an ape". "Choking [in sport] is a result of thinking too much", says Malcolm Gladwell, "panic is a result of thinking too little". It helps to have people around in times of crisis who have been trained to think just enough.

These are essential survival skills. But they need to be deployed with care and an awareness that their time must pass. Eventually we will want to regain our whole selves. Field hospitals and face masks are essential in a state of emergency. But in order to live, to paraphrase Beaudelaire, we also need music and the perfume of flowers. As the immediate crisis unfolds, as the sprint turns into a marathon, so we will start to discern the deeper values at stake, the existential quality of the circumstances we face, the more urgent calls on our conscience. This natural human capacity also needs to be protected and nourished.

The heroic virtues we call on in order to survive will start to give way to the ordinary virtues we need to live, virtues like dignity and care. The distinction is from Todorov's *Facing the Extreme*. Both sets of virtues demand courage and may involve sacrifice, perhaps even of one's life. It is vital for our long-term survival that *both* endure.

Finally, we will come to inhabit the landscape we find ourselves in. This is the Robinson Crusoe moment. The survivors of crisis and upheaval are those who – however slowly – come to terms with the new reality, settle themselves into it, find a way to 'be here now', find their internal centre, the spirit and integrity that gives them reason to live, and from that place begin to plan the long journey home. In the words of Laurence Gonzales, "To survive you must find yourself. Then it won't matter where you are."

GENERATE

FRESH INSIGHT

Lesson Two: Insight

To find ourselves we must make sense of our situation. With awareness we can maintain the energy and intensity that fear has generated, but not descend into panic or denial. Sit in the messiness for a while, recognise we are in unfamiliar territory and generate the one thing that is going to bring us through the crisis – a deep understanding of the meaning of the situation and its potential. In other words, insight.

Insight is a deep, inner understanding that makes new sense of our world, striking us with an 'a-ha' quality, but immediately thereafter feeling obvious. It has the quality Oliver Wendell Holmes Jr was pointing to when he placed such a high value on 'the simplicity beyond complexity'. The simplicity this side of complexity, by contrast, comes cheap and can be misleading. "For every complex human problem there is a solution that is neat, simple and wrong" (H L Mencken).

So - look around. Where are we? What is happening? Three perspectives will help. We must be ready to take a broad view of our circumstances, embracing as much of the complex landscape as possible to gain a systemic appreciation. We must look for the future potential latent in the landscape – a longer-term view of flows and patterns. Cast our gaze forward as well as contemplating what we have lost, seeking a compass bearing to find our way 'home'. And we must remember, always, that we are persons in a human system – and human systems are different.

We know by now that we live in a tightly coupled world, locally and globally, complex in multiple dimensions, in which every action is both a cause and an effect. There are frameworks that allow us to embrace this complexity and straightforward processes for bringing it into play in our decision-making. We should use them.

Bill Sharpe's *Three Horizons* offers a simple framework for appreciating both the unstable patterns of the past and the future potential of the present moment. He encourages us to see at least three patterns of activity: a dominant, managerial, 'business as usual' pattern which has been disrupted by the crisis; an entrepreneurial pattern of innovation and experiment in response; and out on the fringes a pattern of visionary activity, informed by different values from business as usual, holding the promise of a very different future. Bill calls this last 'the patterning of hope'.

It is not only new tools and frameworks we need to thrive in this messiness, confusion and complexity, but also new competencies. The Delors Commission on Education for the 21st Century identified the curriculum back in 1996: learning to be, learning to know, learning to do and learning to live together.

Dancing at the Edge (written with Maureen O'Hara) explores these 21st-century competencies: how to be more and see more in order to thrive and act effectively in the modern world. These competencies are innate: they simply need to be brought to awareness and developed through action. Now is the moment to bring them to the fore.

We can use our psychological literacy to read the familiar human patterns of defensive denial or chaotic collapse in the face of the crisis and then work to support a growth response instead.

We can use our cultural literacy, our awareness that every intervention is a cultural intervention, carrying a culture with it, to be mindful of the cultural impact of the ways we choose to act through the crisis (e.g. calling in the military). We can be alive to the importance of ritual and story in holding a culture together in powerful times.

And we need to tune up our knowledge or epistemic literacy, questioning what counts as 'evidence' in a world where our familiar reference points have disappeared. Sophisticated data modelling offers the false comfort of the 'not yet known' as an apparently rational basis for decision-making. But each of these models will be based on a narrow definition of what counts as valid knowledge and a pattern of assumptions so embedded in our culture as to be almost invisible.

We can become more aware in the crisis of other ways of knowing – from the arts, intuition, poetry, music, the somatic knowledge held in the body, the science of qualities as much as the science of quantities. All of our senses will help round out our appreciation of the present moment.

We may also become aware of more fundamental questions. An existential crisis confronts us with our own mortality. Questions of value, belief and meaning will rise to the surface. Iris Murdoch throws down a strong challenge in her 'polemical sketch' *Against Dryness*. Seeing ourselves as brave and bold individuals, able to impose our will on "an easily comprehended empirical world", is a comforting thought in crisis. Murdoch dismisses it as based on "far too shallow and flimsy an idea of human personality", leaving out the vast hinterland we might call spirit or soul. Protecting ourselves against harm as we come through the crisis is necessary but not sufficient. We also need a reason to live.

Iona Heath likewise urges us to accept vulnerability and risk as intrinsic to our full humanity. As she puts it in her essay *Love's Labours Lost,* "only because we do not understand everything and because we cannot control the future is it possible to live and to be human." There must be room in our observation therefore both for transcendence and contingency.

This is a moment when the kaleidoscope has been shaken. The pieces are in motion and many of us assume they must fall eventually into a new pattern. Surely there can be no 'return to normal' given the frailties and flaws in that system now laid bare?

As noted in the previous chapter, however, people and institutions in a crisis do not automatically transform. They are more likely to double down and, without any necessarily conscious thought, simply become a more intense version of themselves. It is not the removal of cover but this increase in intensity that allows us to see them more clearly. We will have to work hard to maintain our insight once the cover-up resumes.

Harvard economist Dani Rodrik sums up this inconvenient truth well in respect of the current pandemic: "For the most part, the crisis has played out in ways that could have been anticipated from the prevailing nature of governance in different countries. [It] seems to have thrown the dominant characteristics of each country's politics into sharper relief. Countries have in effect become exaggerated versions of themselves.... Rather than putting the world on a significantly different trajectory, it is likely to intensify and entrench already-existing trends".

This is a salutary reminder that wishing does not make it so. If we want a different outcome we will first have to imagine it, and then work for it. Imagination reveals possibility, which is the gateway to hope. We need to read the landscape with all the wisdom we can muster, bringing our own fresh intensity to the task – experiencing what Seamus Heaney in another context called "a moral and imaginative quickening".

And we - this plural, thoughtful, struggling we – will need to grow larger in order to succeed in realising the possibilities we imagine, acting on behalf of those without the power or the physical stamina to bring about transformative change themselves.

This is not 'blue skies' thinking. Insight is grounded in reality – and demands action. That action will in turn bring something new into the world which will attract others and provide the source for new sensemaking and fresh insight. Our first steps will kick start a learning cycle. We cannot plan but we will learn our way out of crisis.

MAINTAIN THE
WILL TO ACT

AND

TO PERSEVERE

Lesson Three: Perseverance

Up to now I have treated 'survival' broadly as a metaphor. But we also know that coming through this crisis will be truly testing. Once the adrenaline wears off, when the emergency relief moves on, when the new normal starts to reveal itself, the pain will be evident – and for some, too much to bear.

Imagination, new thinking and fresh insight are crucial for the future we desire. But so too will be conscious action to look after ourselves, to maintain our energy and persevere, to frame a longer-term story of hope and to care for the wounded.

As a society, we are drawing from a depleted well. The warning signs have been mounting for decades. The World Health Organisation has identified depression as a major source of illness and premature death in the world. Family breakdown, burnout, stress, drink and drug problems, domestic and other violence, accidents at work, absenteeism, addiction, obesity, mental illness and suicide – have become endemic across the world over the last two decades. These are the so-called 'diseases of despair'. We live in powerful times and we are not coping well.

Under the pressure of crisis this picture will be writ large, aggravated by inequality. We will all be more stressed and the burden will fall hardest on the already vulnerable. Some will become depressed, suicides will rise. Others will feel as if they're just 'doing time'. They will be deeply in need of some kind of narrative structure, short- or long-term, that offers a sense of progress, meaning or release, what the literary critic Frank Kermode calls "the sense of an ending".

In the year following the 1929 market crash 23,000 Americans committed suicide, still the highest rate in the US in a single year. Not necessarily Wall St bankers (although there were plenty of them) but farmers who lost their farms, ordinary workers who lost their jobs, entrepreneurs who lost their businesses.

So too today. Once emergency measures to put the economy on life support are withdrawn, we will face a legacy of trauma and despair. The crisis will have consequences.

Ian Mitroff's leading edge work on crisis management in organisations confirms the need to consider the human system, in all its transformative power and all its frailty, in managing our recovery. "You can and will survive – even prosper – but if, and only if, you are prepared emotionally, physically, intellectually, and spiritually."

Mitroff's 'seven essential lessons for surviving disaster' apply equally to individuals, organisations, maybe even societies. They are derived from over 25 years of experience. They point to the fact that even complex organisations can do 'inner work' to build their capacity and resilience.

Most striking is his insistence, in a guide mainly for corporations, on the need for 'right soul'. "Effective crisis management requires a special type of inner spiritual growth," he writes. "Without this, our world is rendered meaningless by a major crisis. Many lose the will to live and regain purpose to their lives… Nothing devastates the soul as much as a crisis."

This must give us pause. When people talk of a crisis of the 'soul', they are talking of a crisis of meaning. It speaks to something beyond the cognitive, our transcendent sense of coherence. We will need to find ways to invite this sense into our conversations in times of crisis. A minute of silence at the start of a meeting provides an opening for it. So too anything that a group considers sacred – music, poetry, beauty – natural rituals of shared simplicity.

The crisis loosens our existential anchors. The natural temptation, both individually and as a system, will be to defend ourselves, retreat to learned behaviours. Or we might go on the attack, lashing out at anything and everything, seeking escape.

We need to hold the crisis. Not to the point where it damages us, but in a way that allows us to acknowledge the new reality, to grieve, avoid both catastrophic and magical thinking, stick with what is real. Celebrate, sing and dance, walk in the woods, enjoy our friends, our family and the dog. Don't despair. If we are in danger of doing so, reach out to someone in a better place. And then, once there is enough self-soothing and stability to tolerate the disturbance, identify the creative edge and move towards growth.

David Bolton, founder of the Centre for Trauma and Transformation in Omagh, Northern Ireland, has a simple message that informs his disaster relief work around the world. "You will recover" he reassures the community, suppressing the passive instinct to wait for rescue. "And the best route to recovery is to help somebody else." It is a natural instinct to want to help, and itself a source of healing.

Think then of the pain of not being able to contribute. Unable to offer our talents when we can see they would be useful. Or witnessing preventable harm, knowing an alternative approach, yet not being able to influence a change of path. In times of crisis, when stakes are raised, the moral pain can become unbearable – and more than overwork is a common cause of burnout.

Maintaining integrity, hanging on to our core, is therefore critical. Joan Didion called it 'moral nerve'. Vaclav Havel, in his classic essay on living under totalitarianism, *The Power of the Powerless,* called it living in truth: "simply straighten your backbone and live in greater dignity as an individual".

This is easier with support. We wrote about dancing *at* the edge, not *on* it. If you can see the edge you are too close – pull back, regroup, live to fight another day. And whatever you do, don't go there alone. If there is somebody else on the end of the rope, you may be able to lean over into the abyss – but there can be no solo climbers. Nobody can be healthy, or resilient, alone. When the air gets thin towards the summit of the mountain, we have nothing to depend on but each other.

The message of this lesson is that we must pay as much attention to our inner resources as we do to the material resources that so preoccupy us at a time of crisis. We all have untold and usually untapped inner resource to manage this transition.

The Brazilian philosopher Roberto Unger reminds us that we experience ourselves as small, finite, vulnerable, decaying organisms. Particularly at this time of global pandemic, we are acutely conscious of this reality.

Yet equally real, and equally pragmatic he insists, is our daily experience of knowing ourselves as gods, with an astounding creative capacity and an infinite imagination. These too are facets of mundane human existence, little attended to at the best of times and usually neglected in a crisis. But they are resources through which, after facing reality and grieving our loss, we will be able to move confidently towards mature hope.

Lesson Four: Hope

And finally comes the poet. So wrote Walter Brueggemann, the Old Testament scholar, about what he called 'the prophetic imagination'.

Writing in the wake of a previous crisis, the attacks on the US on 11 September 2001, he surveyed the landscape revealed and reached his own insight: "9/11 is a symbol and an epitome of the wide and deep loss now faced in our society… that now requires rethinking in a most imaginative way".

"Such rethinking is the work of prophetic imagination… to walk our society into the crisis where it does not want to go, and to walk our society out of that crisis into newness that it does not believe is possible".

Brueggemann describes the role of the prophet as threefold. To warn about the dangers and iniquities of the existing system. To paint a desirable vision of the promised land. And to maintain energy and commitment in the people during the forty years in the wilderness it will take to make the transition. There is a clear echo here of the 'three horizons' frame.

Now, at the moment of crisis, the stakes are raised. The smooth transition to a better future that many of us have imagined is thrown into disarray and confusion. Everything is up for grabs. Rethinking imaginatively or just building back the past lie in the balance. Innovation based on desperation and innovation based on inspiration compete for attention and resource. Underlying assumptions and values rise unexpectedly to the surface in previously pragmatic conversations.

In *Reality, Grief, Hope* Brueggemann explores the enabling conditions for the voice of prophetic imagination to be expressed at such a moment. First, we must embrace the reality of what has occurred and what is revealed. Then we must acknowledge our pain and grieve for what is lost. Only after such preparation can we fashion an authentic hope, a mature hope that is not fantasy or escapism, a hope that engages with reality and despair, a hope that speaks to and springs from our moral core.

The philosopher Jonathan Lear, in his book *Radical Hope – ethics in the face of cultural devastation,* tells the story of Plenty Coups, chief of the Crow nation towards the end of the 19th century. His tribe was coming under pressure from the white man to give up their way of life and enter the reservation. It was a moment of cultural crisis. The bottom dropped out of the Crow nation's world.

Plenty Coups described the transition many years later: "when the buffalo went away the hearts of my people fell to the ground, and they could not lift them up again". As one Crow woman put it: "I am trying to live a life I do not understand".

Some tribes gave in to despair and accepted the white man's superiority – throwing in their lot with 'business as usual'. Resistance was futile. Some – like Sitting Bull and the Sioux – chose violence. They went down fighting – to the bitter end, as it turned out. Neither approach was successful in negotiating a cultural transition.

But Plenty Coups had a dream that although the buffalo would vanish, provided they kept attuned to changing conditions the Crow would come through to find a new way of living. He tapped into "a commitment to the idea that the goodness of the world transcends one's limited and vulnerable attempts to understand it."

Lear calls this *'radical hope'* - the hope for cultural rebirth, but without any clear understanding of what that will look like in practice. In the event Crow youth learned the white man's law, negotiated favourable settlements, maintained far more of their land than any other tribe and came to reinvent notions of honour and courage in a world without warriors.

Lear writes: "There may be various forms of ethical criticism that one might be tempted to level at this form of hopefulness: that it was too complacent; that it didn't face up to the evil that was being inflicted on the Crow tribe. But it is beyond question that the hope was a remarkable human accomplishment – in no small part because it avoided despair".

Like every serious student of hope, Lear emphasises that it is a muscular virtue, a courageous achievement in the face both of its opposite - despair, and of its pale imitation – self-delusion. Hope is a source of strength, 'the courage of our convictions', "an axe you break down doors with in an emergency" (Rebecca Solnit).

It is strong because it is grounded. It intends what the imagination has first seen as possible. We can dream of or desire but we cannot *hope* for something that is impossible or even unreasonable. Terry Eagleton's forensic study *Hope Without Optimism* points out that when we ask "Is there any hope?" we can only really mean "Is it reasonable to hope?". There is always a cognitive element, always a basis in reason. "You can feel afraid without any conception of what it is you fear; but you cannot feel a passionate longing for something of which you can give no account at all."

The evidence for hope is essential and always there to be found. Robust hope offers present signs of its future fulfilment, even if only at a small scale. It is a home in which we can "take up residence" (Solnit again). Paul Ricoeur concludes: "Hope is a passion for the possible".

Possible, but not certain. Just as doubt is a necessary component of faith, so there is no hope without the possibility of failure. Optimism and pessimism, by contrast, are certain and unequivocal. They assume the future is assured, either positively or negatively, and hence rob us of agency.

To say 'I am an optimist' is like saying 'I am left-handed': it has nothing to say about the true state of the world or its potential. The point about whether we declare the glass half-empty or half-full is that the reality of the situation is immaterial to the answer. Eagleton, echoing Rollo May and many others before him, describes optimism – a blind faith that everything will turn out for the best – as "the enemy of hope".

Hope is active, shaping a future that is open and could still go either way. We need the courage to act, but also the humility to risk failure. Don Michael urges 'tentative commitment': "Be willing to look at a situation carefully enough, to risk enough, to contribute enough effort, enough hope, to undertake your project... and to recognise that we might have it wrong. We may have to back off or change not only how we are doing something but whether to do it at all". When we say that we 'hope' to achieve something, rather than that we 'will', we are admitting we may not succeed. Augustine wrote that hope "is given to the humble".

Eagleton notices the renewal in Shakespeare's late comedies, redemption often achieved with the aid of grace, art, magic and miracle. "Left to their own devices, history and politics appear unlikely to usher in the New Jerusalem. You need to stray beyond those domains – to the countryside, a remote island, the common people, myth and fairy tale, the restorative cycles of Nature, the younger generation, the regenerative power of the ocean – for the resources that might renew them". In other words, we must use our imagination.

And then we must act - "put our hands on the arc of history and bend it again toward the hope of a better day" (President Obama's victory speech in 2008, echoing Martin Luther King). Put simply, we need to find among us the individuals and organisations willing to connect their actions today to a vision that is more than a patched-up version of the past. These are the pioneers.

They display all the characteristics I speak of in these pages. They are not waiting to be rescued. They are aware of the larger, shifting context for their actions. They can read the changing landscape and know when to move, when to hold back, how to pick their way through unknown territory. They are not afraid of big thoughts and wide ambition. They have strong values that feed their capacity to persevere through good times and bad. They show moral nerve and stand for the ordinary virtues of dignity and care. They provide inspiration to others.

In other words, they are human – just like you and me. It is vital that we also find this capacity in ourselves and support it in each other if we are to flourish amidst the worst of what may yet lie ahead. This is, and has always been, the true source of radical hope – and the way we can turn it into reality.

Further Reading

Introduction – Practical Hope
Leicester, Graham (2020) *Transformative Innovation* (2nd ed),
Triarchy Press

Lesson One: Survival
Gonzales, Laurence (2005) *Deep Survival*, W.W. Norton
Todorov, Tzvetan (1997) *Facing the Extreme*, Henry Holt

Lesson Two: Insight
Hodgson, Anthony (2012) *Ready for Anything*, Triarchy Press

Sharpe, Bill (2020) *Three Horizons* (2nd ed), Triarchy Press

O'Hara, Maureen and Leicester, Graham (2019) *Dancing at the Edge* (2nd ed), Triarchy Press

Michael, Don (1997) *On Learning to Plan and Planning to Learn* (2nd ed), Miles River Press

Murdoch, Iris (1999) 'Against Dryness' in *Existentialists and Mystics: Writings on Philosophy and Literature*, Penguin

Lesson Three: Perseverance
Kermode, Frank (1968) *The Sense of an Ending*, Oxford University Press

Mitroff, Ian (2005) *Why Some Companies Emerge Stronger and Better from a Crisis,* Amacom

Unger, Roberto (2009) *The Self Awakened,* Harvard University Press

Havel, Václav (1985) *The Power of the Powerless*, Routledge

Lesson Four: Hope

Brueggemann, Walter (2001) *The Prophetic Imagination,* Fortress Press

Brueggemann, Walter (2014) *Reality, Grief, Hope,* Wm. B. Eerdmans Publishing

Lear, Jonathan (2008) *Radical Hope*, Harvard University Press

Solnit, Rebecca (2016) *Hope in the Dark,* Haymarket Books

Eagleton, Terry (2015) *Hope Without Optimism*, Yale University Press

Author Notes

Graham Leicester is a founder and Director of IFF. He previously ran Scotland's leading think tank, the Scottish Council Foundation, founded in 1997. From 1984 to1995 he served as a diplomat in HM Diplomatic Service, specializing in China (he speaks Mandarin Chinese) and the EU. Between 1995 and 1997 he was senior research fellow with the Constitution Unit at University College London.

He has also worked as a freelance professional cellist, including with the BBC Concert Orchestra. He has strong interests in governance, innovation, education and human development and has previously worked with OECD, the World Bank Institute and other agencies on the themes of governance in a knowledge society and the governance of the long term.

graham@internationalfuturesforum.com

Jennifer Williams is critically acclaimed at making hand-made books, cutouts, photographs, illustrations, prints and puppets. She is a trustee and member of International Futures Forum and for 31 years directed the Centre for Creative Communities.

About IFF

IFF (International Futures Forum) is a non-profit organization established in 2001 to support a transformative response to complex and confounding challenges and to restore the capacity for effective action in today's powerful times.

At its heart is a deeply informed inter-disciplinary and international learning community of individuals from a range of backgrounds covering diverse perspectives, countries and disciplines. Over many years this group has generated a series of powerful insights and concepts which have been progressively tested in practice with business, governments and communities.

This learning is brought together in the practice of transformative innovation for system transition. It is IFF's mission both to continue refining the practice in light of experience and to make the tools, processes, attitudes, frameworks and conceptual breakthroughs that support it as widely available as possible – fostering practical hope and wise initiative.

International Futures Forum, Aberdour, Scotland

www.internationalfuturesforum.com

www.iffpraxis.com

About Triarchy Press

Triarchy Press is an independent publisher of books that
bring a wider, systemic or contextual approach to many
different areas of life, including:

Government, Education, Health and other public services

Innovation, the Future and Future Studies

Ecology, Sustainability and Regenerative Cultures

Leading and Managing Organisations

The Money System

Psychotherapy and Arts and other Expressive Therapies

Walking, Mythogeography, Movement and Somatics

For details of other IFF titles and for books by
Nora Bateson, Daniel Wahl, Russ Ackoff, Barry Oshry, John
Seddon, Phil Smith, Bill Tate, Patricia Lustig, Sandra Reeve,
Nelisha Wickremasinghe, Alyson Hallett and other
remarkable writers, please visit:

www.triarchypress.net